# Fun with Gel Markers

by Jennifer Flanagan

W9-BKV-167

## Contents

Scholastic Inc.

New York   Toronto   London   Auckland   Sydney   Mexico City   New Delhi   Hong Kong   Buenos Aires

# ◉ Get Ready to Create with Gel Markers! ◉

**Dear Young Artist,**

Create artwork that glows! Use your gel markers, along with your imagination, to make some really awesome effects on dark paper. Your pictures will practically pop off the page. Have fun!

**Dear Parent,**

Gel markers are perfect for making nighttime scenes and for creating fantasy drawings. Children have such a gift of imagination! I hope you enjoy sharing in your child's creativity.

*Jennifer*

## Tips for Working with Gel Markers

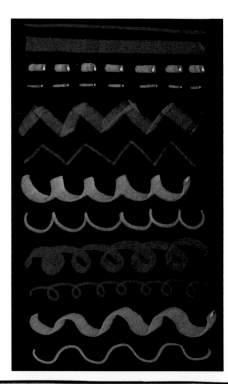

1. Spread out newspaper before you start, just in case you draw off the edges of your paper.

2. You can draw lightly in pencil first, if you like.

3. Use the tips of your markers to draw thin lines, and the sides of your markers to make thick lines.

4. Be sure to put the caps back on your markers when you're finished using them so they don't dry out.

## 🕷 Wacky Web 🕷

How does a spider spin its web? Let's make one and find out!

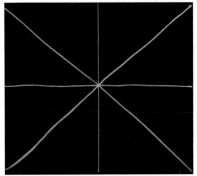

1. Use your white gel marker to make an X from corner to corner on your paper. Then crisscross the X in the center.

2. Now make eight curving lines around the center of the web, connected to each other. Keep moving out from the center, connecting lines over and over, until the web is full.

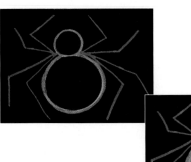

3. Next, draw the spider that's spinning the web! Start with a circle for the spider's body. Add a smaller circle for the head, and draw eight bent legs. Give your spider eyes, and color its body.

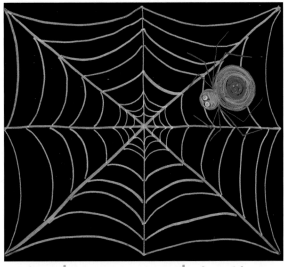

Most spiders move around at night. Turn the page to make a nighttime garden!

#  Nighttime in the Garden

You can explore a garden after dark. What might you see?

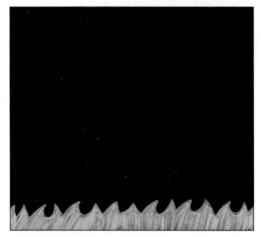

1. Make some spiky grass across the bottom of your paper.

2. Draw tulips, daisies, and a bunch of other colorful flowers.

3. How about adding a branch of a white birch tree?

4. Some sparkly stars and a moon in the nighttime sky are next.

5. Can you find some critters hiding in the garden? Draw pairs of yellow eyes all over the ground. Look, there's your spider, hiding in the garden!

## Here's More!

Whoooo do you see in the tree? If you like, add an owl to your garden scene.

What else can you find in your garden? How about your favorite fruits and veggies? Turn the page to see!

# Fruits and Veggies

Draw some colorful fruits and veggies that look almost good enough to eat.

1. Make a long, skinny banana and color it in.

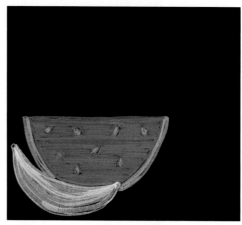

2. Use your green marker to draw a half circle for a watermelon rind. Draw a magenta line across the top, connecting the two ends of the rind. Add seeds. Color the rest of your watermelon.

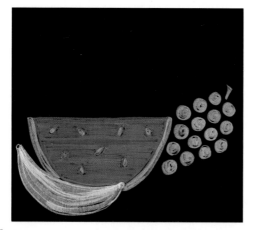

3. Draw a big bunch of green circles for grapes and add a stem.

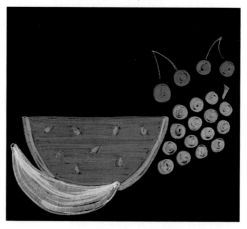

4. Draw some cherries. Add long green stems to each pair.

5. Make a purple oval for a plum and a circle for an apple. Color them both. Use yellow to draw oval-like shapes for lemons.

6. Don't forget your veggies! How about adding broccoli, string beans, and carrots?

What a nice bunch of fruits and veggies! Can you pick some flowers from your garden, too? Turn the page to see.

#  Fancy Flowers

Pick the fanciest flowers from your garden, and put them in a bright vase.

1. Make a curvy vase of any size or style you like.

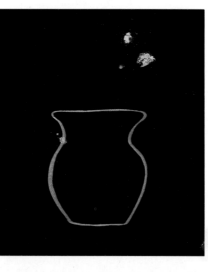

2. Decorate your vase with bright colors.

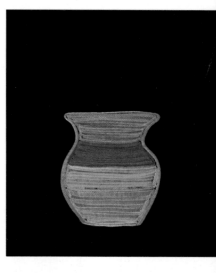

3. Start your flowers by making green stems that come out of the vase in all directions.

4. Draw a line behind your vase for a table. Color your table.

**5.** Use bright colors to draw some big flower petals of different sizes and shapes. Make an assortment of colorful blooms.

What colorful flowers might you find in the rain forest? Turn the page to see!

# Rain Forest

Can you find the snake and the butterfly hiding in this jungle?

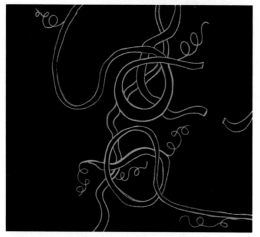

1. Use your green marker to draw lots of loopy vines in the center of your paper.

2. Add all sorts of different leaves and flowers, too.

3. *Hisssss...* is that a vine or a slithery snake? Give your snake an eye and a tongue.

4. Butterflies are fun to draw. Make the butterfly's body, wings, and feelers in a light outline.

**5.** Some butterflies have eyeball patterns on their wings to scare off predators. Make these special patterns on your butterfly's wings, or color your butterfly any way you like.

## Here's More!

A toucan is a tropical bird with a really large beak. Can you make a colorful toucan beak poking out from behind a big leaf?

Imagine soaring in the sky like your toucan. Turn the page to see how!

# WHAT A VIEW!
## ☀ Hot-air Balloons ☀

Have you ever seen a hot-air balloon? It can soar way up above the treetops!

1. Choose any color marker to draw a big rectangular or square balloon basket. Add a pattern on your basket.

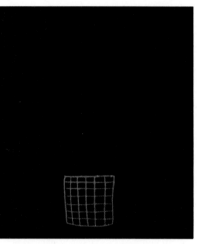

2. Use your white marker to draw a big balloon above your basket. Add ropes hanging down from the balloon, attached to your basket.

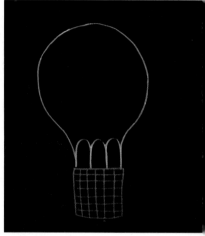

3. Make more balloons that are smaller to show that they are farther away.

4. Use your boldest markers to color designs or patterns on your balloons.

5. Would you like to add some soaring M-shaped seagulls next to your balloons? How about some puffy clouds and a sun?

What kind of view do you have from your hot-air balloon? Turn the page to see!

 # Bird's-eye View

Have you ever wanted a view like a bird has when it's flying up above?

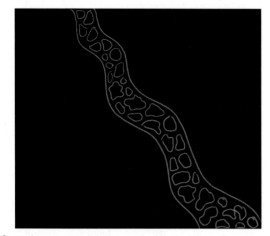

1. What would a park look like from the sky? First draw a path through the park as seen from above. Fill it in with stones.

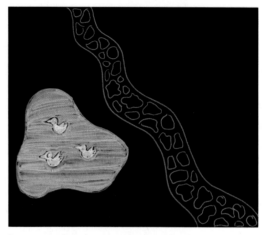

2. Draw a blob-shape to make your pond. Add a few yellow ducks. Now, color in your pond.

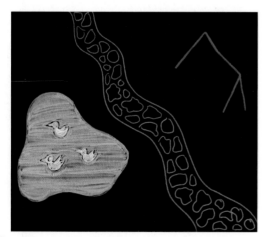

3. Draw a frame for a swing set.

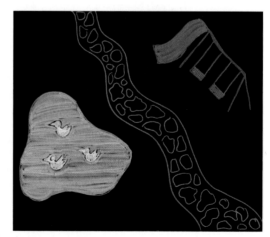

4. Add a slide and a couple of swings for you and your friends.

5. What else do you see from up above?
   How about grass and treetops?

Can you soar even higher than a bird or a hot-air balloon? Turn the page to zoom into outer space!

# ❄ Space Voyage ❄

Which planet would you like to visit?
Let's create a spaceship for this adventure!

1. In one corner of your sheet of paper, draw part of a circle for the Earth. Color it blue and green for water and land.

2. For the spaceship, begin with a long, skinny triangle shape. Draw a line through the middle to divide it into two skinnier triangles. Add some triangle wings.

3. Draw oval-shaped jet motors on the bottom of your spaceship. Make fire blast out of the jets.

4. Add round windows and designs to your spaceship.

**5.** Stars complete your sky and picture.

**Here's More!** You can add other planets to your outer space scene.

Where does the spaceship land when it returns to Earth? How about the ocean? Turn the page to see!

# Land Ahoy!

Pretend you're in a ship, looking out a porthole window. What do you see?

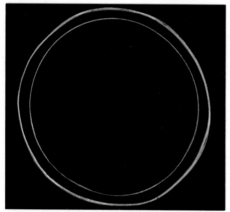

1. Draw the biggest circle possible on your paper. You may want to trace a round object, like a coffee can or a plate. Add a slightly smaller circle inside the first circle. That's your porthole!

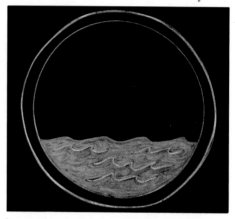

2. Draw a wavy water line across the lower part of your smaller circle. Use your blue and white markers to color in the ocean and its waves.

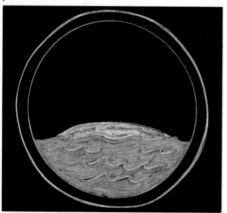

3. What do you see? It's land—straight ahead! With your yellow marker, draw an island, curving out above the ocean.

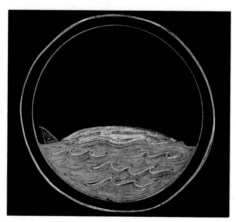

4. Add a fin sticking out of the water. Is that a dolphin or a shark?

5. How about including some tropical palm trees? Start with a large tree trunk, and add big, green palm leaves. Make a bright sun and some birds soaring in the sky.

Imagine that a make-believe creature lives on this island. What might it look like? Turn the page to see!

# FANTASY FUN
## Crazy Creature

It's animal mix-and-match time! Here are some ideas to choose from:

| | | | |
|---|---|---|---|
| Butterfly wings | Flamingo legs | Lion's mane | Snake tongue |
| Camel's hump | Giraffe neck | Pig nose | Toucan beak |
| Duck feet | Insect antennae | Rabbit ears | Walrus tusks |
| Fish scales | Leopard spots | Raccoon eyes | Zebra stripes |

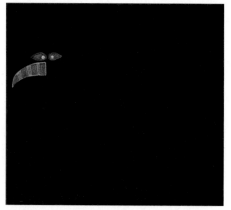

1. Start with a nose and eyes.

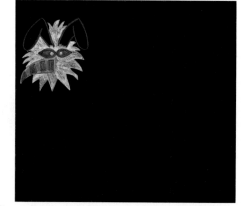

2. Add a mane and some floppy ears, if you like.

3. Now for the neck and body!

4. Give your creature legs and feet.

5. What else can you add to your critter? Antennae or wings? Fish scales?

Does your crazy creature have a name? Try combining the names of all the different animals you used into one.

This crazy creature looks pretty silly, doesn't it? Now let's make a silly face. Turn the page to see!

# 👁 Freaky Faces 👁

## Let's mix-and-match, and use some bright and wacky colors!

1. Begin with a large egg-shaped or oval-shaped face. The smaller end will be the chin.

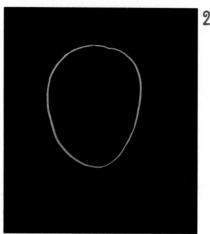

2. Add a neck and shoulders that go off the bottom of the page. Draw a necklace or a fancy shirt collar.

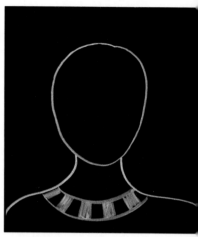

3. Draw a wavy line down the center of the face for a long, weird nose facing sideways.

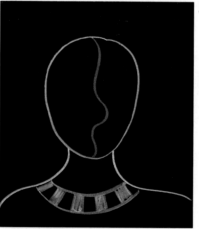

4. Have you ever seen ears on a cheek or forehead? Draw ears in different places. Don't forget to add eyes. How about mixing up the colors?

5. What else is goofy about your freaky face? Draw a colorful mouth and cheeks. Add some freckles.

6. Give your odd face some wild hair. It can be short and spiky, or long and curly, or both.

This mixed-up face is pretty funny, isn't it?

What else can you dream up? Turn the page to see!

# 👑 Sweet Dreams 👑

Draw one of your favorite nighttime dreams in a "dream bubble."

1. Start by drawing your head. Make a half circle for your face. Add hair, eyes, a nose, and a mouth.

2. Draw a rectangular shape around your head for a pillow. Make a blanket to cover you up.

3. Add a bed post on each side of your pillow.

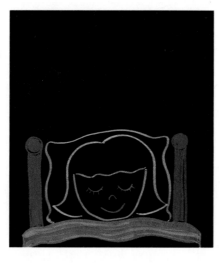

4. Draw a big bubble and three smaller bubbles coming from your sleeping head.

5. Add your dream inside
   the big bubble shape.

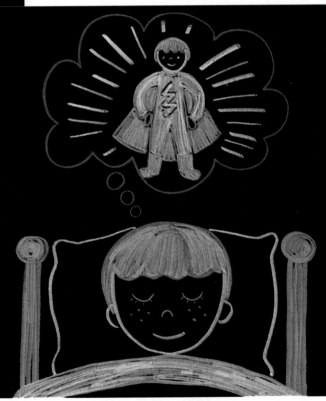

Next, let's dream up an imaginary vehicle that can take
you anywhere you want to go! Turn the page to see.

# ❁ Fantasy Flight ❁

You can mix-and-match from many real vehicles to create a make-believe one!

| | | | |
|---|---|---|---|
| Bicycle | Helicopter | Race car | Skateboard |
| Bus | Inline skates | Sailboat | Submarine |
| Car | Jeep | Scooter | Truck |
| Go-cart | Plane/Jet | Ship | |

1. To make the body of your vehicle, start with a shape like a rectangle or a square, and add a triangle.

2. Draw windows. Color in your vehicle.

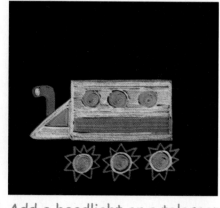

3. Add a headlight or a telescope. Do you want large or small tires?

4. To make your vehicle fly or float, add propellers or any other parts you like!

**5.** How about adding a triangle sail?
Color stripes or any pattern you like.

Can your vehicle fly, drive
in the water, or both?

What else can you dream up? Turn the page to see!

# ✸ My 3-D Candy Dream House ✸

Something 3-D—or three-dimensional—doesn't look flat on paper.

1. To make a house 3-D, we need to show two sides. Start by drawing two squares like this.

2. Add a triangle and a square for your roof. Draw a chimney that looks like a gumdrop next.

3. Add a candy door and candy windows.

4. Draw a walkway made out of gumdrops, too!

5. Add lollipop flowers in the yard.

What special toys might you have in your dream house? Turn the page to see!

# Toys, Toys, Toys!

Imagine all your favorite toys lined up on a shelf!

**To make a shelf:**

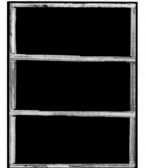

Start with a rectangular shape. Add two lines across the middle to make shelves. This will be your toy shelf.

**To make blocks:**

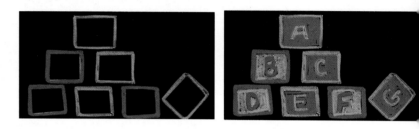

Make a row of squares and add more rows on top. To one side, make a block that fell off the pile. Write letters on your blocks, and color them.

**To make a teddy bear:**

1. Start with a circle for a face and add two half circles for ears. Make two ovals for the teddy bear's front paws and two larger ovals for its hind paws.

2. Draw lines for the teddy bear's arms and legs.

3. Now add a curved line for the bear's belly. Give your bear eyes, a nose, and a little smile.

**To make a skateboard:**

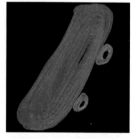

Draw a long oval shape for your skateboard. Add two wheels. Color your skateboard.

To make a soccer ball:

1. Use your white gel marker to trace something 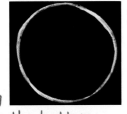 round, like the bottom of a drinking glass.

2. Draw a six-sided shape in the center of the  circle. Make six lines connecting the points of the shape to the edge of your ball.

3. Use your white marker and  another marker to color in your ball.

Add more balls to your toy collection, if you like.

Are you ready to play?

31

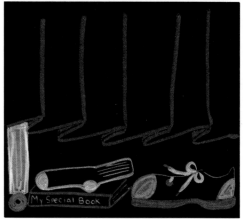

## My Name in Lights

What makes you *you*? Make a poster with your name in the center in neon letters. Add short, sparkling lines around your name. Include your favorite words and drawings of what makes you happy, such as your hobbies, friends, or feelings.

## What's Under Your Bed?

Are you missing a sock, shoe, or favorite book? Maybe you should check under your bed! Make a wavy line in the middle of your page for a sheet or blanket. Draw a sock lying on the floor with a shoe next to it. Add a book, too, or whatever else you might find under your bed!

ISBN 0-439-33624-4

Designed and illustrated by Julie Mullarkey-Gnoy

*Toys, Toys, Toys!* and *What's Under Your Bed?* illustrated by Melanie S. George

12 11 10 9 8 7 6 5 4 3                                   4 5 6 7/0
Printed in the U.S.A.
First Scholastic printing, June 2002